M. S.

Old castles, Including Sketches of Carlisle, Corby, and Linstock Castles

M. S.

Old castles, Including Sketches of Carlisle, Corby, and Linstock Castles

ISBN/EAN: 9783744730068

Printed in Europe, USA, Canada, Australia, Japan

Cover: Foto ©ninafisch / pixelio.de

More available books at **www.hansebooks.com**

OLD CASTLES:

INCLUDING SKETCHES

OF

CARLISLE, CORBY, and LINSTOCK

CASTLES;

WITH A POEM ON CARLISLE.

By M. S.

AUTHOR OF AN ESSAY ON SHAKESPEARE, ETC.

"It is in the soul that architecture exists." —*Emerson.*

CARLISLE :

GEORGE COWARD, SCOTCH STREET.

MDCCCLXVIII.

The following, to some extent incomplete and un-finished sketches of "Old Castles," were written three or four years ago, and one of them appeared in the *Border Magazine*, for which the sketch of Carlisle Castle was also written, but owing to the failure of the magazine it did not appear. It was afterwards printed in two consecutive numbers of the *Carlisle Express*, and some who saw it there for the first time were kind enough to say that it deserved a better place—that it was a mistake to allow it to appear in a newspaper at all. Feeling that there was some truth in these remarks, the author concluded to reprint the whole of them in the more permanent and more availabe form of a book, which while it may perhaps serve as a hand-book to strangers and others, may at the same time perhaps serve also to enlarge to some small extent the general appreciation of places whose eventful histories comprehend so much of the general history of the past, and which ought as a result to be sources of interest and instruction to the localities in which they stand.

M. S.

CARLISLE,
March 31, 1868.

CONTENTS.

CARLISLE.

CAREL! O canny Carel of the past,
　　How sweetly flow the streams that bound
　　　　thee round:
The Eden fair, upon whose waves are cast
Thy oft repeated chimes—a pleasant sound
To the worn wanderer on its rock-bound sides;
And, east and west, its affluents, whose soft tides,
Flow where they will, are still with beauty crowned.
And every beck and little streamlet found,
Or far or near thy fell-bound precincts round,
Has something more, a something quite apart
From every other streamlet, the great heart
Of Nature, in her freest fairest moods,
Throbs in their flow, and fills their solitudes.
Beauteous for ever! Time on them has laid
No trace of age or change; they brightly fall
As glide the seasons, either swift or staid,
As when the Roman cohorts fierce and tall
First made these valleys ring with Latian sounds.
And everywhere about them still abounds
Their virgin beauty, by the years unspoiled.
Art's modern wonder, which no more astounds,
(Showing the heights to which the world has toiled.)

But adding grace to grace, and charm to charm,
Its viaducts most rare across them spanned,
And linking field to field, and farm to farm—
The ornaments of all the pleasant land—
But heightening what at first they seemed to harm,
Beauty with beauty still delighting well.
    But thou hast more, O Carlisle, than thy streams!
Thy castled heights crown many a charming rood,
Renowned in olden story; field and fell,
Through many a league of gracious solitude,
Where yet perchance some genuine bard still dreams,
Bearing sure witness to the ancient feud
Of Scot and Briton, and the Roman strength
That interposed between them, and subdued
The vagrant Pict to British force at length.
And age by age the gathering centuries round,
Thy history's written still upon the ground,
Which compasses thee around, or far or near,
The travelled wanderer catching something here
To-day, if skilful, of the ancient sound,
Of the fierce strife of Saxon and of Gael,
Which through long centuries kept thee desolate.
And intermixed with these of far off date,
Wrought in with antique zeal, flows many a tale
Of Dane and Druid, and the famous state
In which King Arthur kept his Yule feast here.
Nor is there wanting in the grammary
Of that far age, the names of holier fame,
Or tales of purer import; where we dwell
Within these walls, the holy Cuthbert came,
The guest of Egfrid, visiting the well—
True relic of the times—the Romans made;

And Ermengard, his friend and faithful aid,
The wife of Egfrid, here wrought piously,
Herself and sister—names which through the shade
Of many storms and centuries still run free.
    And, all about, tradition decks thee out,
This castled county, rich in antique lore,
Bearing on all its face the land about
Strange tales of wonder of the times of yore.
Here may be heard sublimely from the past
The voices old of heroes and of kings—
The Bruce and Wallace, and, not least, though last,
Cromwell, who caught their spirit, and who flings
An air of health o'er British rule to-day.
And, joined with these their fellows in the fray,
Circling thy walls to-day the echo rings
Of Norman and Plantagenet, and the array
Of armies vast, whom Scotia's Bard still sings,
Though he, with his immortal Marmion,
A traveller here, long since has passed away.
Nor must we quite forget the lady fair
Who hither came a queen without a crown—
The royal Mary, yet most desolate ;
Her hopes from their high altitude cast down,
And burd'ning all her spirit with the weight
Such ruin brings, of wild tumultuous care.
Her name is linked to thine, O Carlisle, still
Linked with thy ancient walls, thy castle old ;
Linked with thy bounds from far, o'er vale and hill,
Piercing their deeps and distance manifold,
Her vision wandered ; Caledonia wild,
Home of her heart, her childhood's airy nest,
Winning her bosom soft, by pride beguiled,

To longings once again for its true rest,
To thoughts of peace, perchance by crowns unspoiled.
She was thy captive sad, this lady fair,
And thou hadst many captives in those days,
Noteless and notable ; thy dungeons old,
Close cavern'd in from all the sun's sweet rays,
And all devoid of lightest breath of air,
Have borne upon their basements dank and cold
The wearying form of many a child of care.
    Here came the Jacobite still unsubdued,
A patriot brave, and all devoid of fear,
His heart still rising, neither chain nor cell
His hopes despoiling ; long the terror here
Of all this Border Country, his old feud
Oft ending in vast file on Gallows Hill,
As did the brave Mc.Donald, long renowned
As the Mc.Ivor of the Scottish tale.
And in these times, and often with these found,
Nor short of them in resolution hale,
Was the moss trooper––brigand most profound,
Yet something more than brigand all the while.
His was the feud of races ; clan with clan—
Stern hater of the British name and isle.
His mode of action still the good old plan,
That they should take who have the greatest power,
And they who can should keep—a rule which wrought
Full often his own ruin ; hour by hour
O'er field and fell and moorland waste and wild
The war note rising, and the blood-hounds' yell.
Such were the means the troubled country sought
To capture him ; and often he was brought
In chainéd bands, to die in durance here ;

Or, standing through slow months, from earth exiled,
At last to perish on some gibbet near.
   Sad were those times for thee, O Carlisle, then
Thy battlements and towers and gates all o'er
Were clothed with blanching skulls and features fair,
Distorted by the halter, fixed as when
Death did his solemn deed, were left to glare
On the meek face of all thy unstained life.
Yet with this rigour stern thou hadst no rest,
Still were thy gates the scenes of martial strife,
Nor didst thou prosper; war is still unblest;
Its crown is still a ruin, and its knife
Is still insatiate, moving in death's sphere
A track of desolation. Many a tear
Has orphaned sorrow, blasted by its fate,
Shed in thy walls; and weeping women here,
Spared by its doom, left lorn and desolate,
Have sunk insensibly to early death
(Of love deprived, seeking no other mate);
And age, bereft by it, its straitened breath
Has here drawn all alone uncomforted.
Such are war's tragic fortunes; and more drear,
Could the great past arise, and, through its dead,
Tell all the horrid tale, would they appear.
Here in thy gates of eld, war's fiery sphere,
Have horrors dread been done, to shock the light,
And make the stars recoil the living day,
Polluted by them, and the holy night
By them all scared and tortured with mad fear.
Think for one instant of the frightful deed
Ohanging twelve fair boys in open day,
In one dread cluster, without stain or crime,

Because their sires, perchance by some foul play,
Had failed to ransom them in their sore need
As their own hostages, at the just time.
Or think again of some fair lady's form,
With hands all jewelled, and soft silken tire,
Enclosed in mortar, while the young blood warm,
Wandered within it, and its eyes' pure fire
Still kept its native lustre unbedimmed.
These things are sad; but here, as though o'er-brimmed,
Just at their verge two nations' wrath run o'er,
And cruelty ran riot, centring all its strength
Upon this city's borders, till at length
Change soothed time's temper, and, from shore to shore,
The twain became one kingdom, never more
To rage together, but henceforth to be
Helpers together in the world's great fight
For peace, for freedom, and for amity;
And, above all, for progress, and the right
Man claims of man, has in his nature free
To use the privileges and gifts of light.

Such is thy past, O Carlisle, yet things fair,
Brave deeds, and noble, large enduring life
Have been its firm attendants; wise and well,
Heroic still through all that age long strife,
Thy sires have borne them and this Border air
With all that nature owns of rare most rife,
Has borne upon its currents the sweet swell
Of Piety calm hearted, and of prayer,
And sweet domestic kindness. "Belted Will,"
The best known name of all of Border fame,
Was a most tender lover, where his heart
Had tender dues and duties to fulfil,

In his own castle, where his husband's part
Was played out with a zeal that gladdens still,
Worthy his Howard blood, his Howard name.
    And here have Science and sweet Poesy,
Born of the soul despoilers still of ill,
Hung out their purer ensigns, the old wound
Of sorrow healing with the pleasant thrill
Of native harmony, whose modern round
Poor Anderson essayed, nor without skill,
To trance the native heart with native thought,
And give it back the life it erst had found
In Cumbria's homely pleasures, all unfraught
With the soft manners of an age refined.
    But Blamire did this best ; her woman's mind,
Soul of her song, its burden's tender type,
Blent with her native lyre the touch and tone
Of purer genius ; and her numbers ripe
All up and down this Border country strewn,
Have pierced the deeps of Cumbria's gentler heart,
Refining it to virtue ; and her song,
Sung here in pleasant guise with her sweet friend,
The gentle Gilpin, who in all had part,
Will in these hills and valleys linger long,
And cheer the native Cumbrian to the end.
    Nor has there failed the bard of loftier fame ;
For Wordsworth here, of Eden eloquent,
Sang as the poet should, with the true swell
Of a true heart, wrapt in its own intent ;
The castled cliff, the craggy hill and dell,
All loud with voice of streams of Cumbrian frame,
Still gave his muse content, and here he found
His spirit still inspired, where'er he went.

Nor has this city, in still older times,
Wanted its singer ; "Carel" still has been
The theme of song, the burden of old rhymes,
The quickening word of numbers rashly wrought,
Giving its living spirit to the sheen
Of all the Poet's music and his thought.
Here 'twas lived Percy, who o'erwrought by love
Of Border Minstrelsy, around it threw
A band protecting, gathering a sweet store
Of all its beauties, neither scarce nor few,
For common delectation, which he wove
Into his " Reliques "—songs which here of yore
Out of the people's common customs grew.
So sanctified by song has all thy past,
Fierce though it seems, been shaped to something true,
Its rigours and its sorrows brought at last,
As doth the storm cloud in the rainbow's hue,
To minister to pleasure, and create
Another mind, which, on the future cast,
Shall ripen into power, and subdue
War, and war's spirit, either soon or late.
　　And still, still other names await my line ;
Thy race of bards, O Carlisle, still flows on—
Thy last and latest, Lonsdale, of his sires,
The Border Poets, a most worthy son.
He sleeps too soon ; but still his numbers pure,
Fraught with the love that 'mongst these mountains
　　　　grows,
Shall still be honoured, still from door to door,
Spread the sweet sympathy that through them flows.
　　And thou hast had thy Paley, clear and strong,
Not quite a poet, but poetical :

He fed his thought thy ancient towers among,
Making it clear and simple, of a fall
That catches common hearing. Well he wrote,
And in the lists of fame his name is filed—
A Theologic Wordsworth, who took note
How God in all the world Himself has soul'd.
He sleeps in thy cathedral, 'mong the dust
Of many noble fathers, whose pure fame
Is its best consecration, and whose hearts,
Still mingling with its worship, light the flame
Of pure devotion, where the heart's strong trust,
One with their own in its pure heavenward aim,
The letter from the spirit wisely parts,
Finding the eternal substance, the bright Name
In which all worship centres, and all rest.
  Nor in these spheres alone hast thou been blest,
Thy stock's been fruitful in a varied life,
Varied, yet kindred ; the same generous fires
Have run through all thy heroes, the old strife
Finding new objects, as the changing times
Have changed in their ambitions, giving zest
For things more purely noble—Art and Thought,
Destined to lead the world a purer way,
And ransom it from evil, consecrate
With all the true pure life religion yields.
So the brave artist, Watson, crowned thy state—
A lowly boy, inspired by Art's pure ray—
Bringing fresh garlands from her fairy field,
To honour thy old walls, thy towers grey,
Flushing afresh with the new vivid light
Of the world's onward genius, and his own.
Peace to his memory ! He was a true knight

Of worthy labour ; and his name, deep sown
In thy now peaceful annals, the low sight
Of youth irresolute, in sloth upgrown,
May lead to purer vision ; all his thought
Imbuing with the sense of the vast power
There lives in man, as man—a power fraught
With life to quicken every passing hour
Into divinest action, and to speed—
Such is the substance of the human flower—
Even in the lowliest mind, ambition's seed.

Nor must the Muse forget the gentle Steel,
Who in the ranks of genius, Mentor mild,
Marshall'd the powers of progress rising here,
With Journalistic Science ; prone to feel
How vast earth's bondage from those powers exiled,
How great earth's sorrows when usurped by fear.
He rose by effort to the worthiest fame ;
One of the people, a brave son of toil,
Whose heart aspiring unto knowledge bound,
Was quickened into hope by its pure flame,
Spreading at length its fruit o'er all the soil
Of this fair country, all the Border round.

So flows thy list of worthies—not half done—
A list too long for such a line as this ;
For thou than these, of daughter and of son,
Hast boasted many ; and thy sires I wis
Could tell of thy renowned ones without end,
Fostering their pride and thine with every word,
And every word a truth, for virtue lies
In a green covert, whose fair boughs, soft stirred
With only its own breath, no motions lends
To the loud trumpeting which through the skies

With names of noisier note and honours blends.
Who knows who's honoured thee? Who's made thee
    strong?
Who's lifted up thy head and made thee great?
What prayer or speech or unremembered song
Has helped the current of thy life's new date.
Here influences have wrought, untold, unknown,
The holy breath of thought, that never grew
Into a verbal framing; the dear love
Which but the heart that held it ever knew;
The hope which brings true rest, the peace that's wove
Into domestic manners pure and free,
Blessing the inner spirit; far above,
In its unnoted strength, the ecstasy
Of joys of grander import, its soft tone
Working in ways of good continually,
Soothing the sighs of grief, and pain's shrill groan,
And healing the vexed heart of poverty.
    These, and a thousand more of gentler force,
Sweet influences in thine own heart upgrown,
Powers all ignored by fame, their silent course
Keeping unseen around life's common day,
Into thy deeper soul a charm have thrown,
Keeping it even in the grander way
Of Public Progress and of Modern Life.
    So hast thou grown illumined by the ray—
Deep in thy bosom still, through all thy strife—
The ray of heavenly wisdom, whose soft sway
Has changed thy destinies, thy spirit rife
With old barbaric hate, and wrought in thee
The life and purpose of a city free.
Henceforth thy path is onward. Victory

Is thine in other fields than those of blood ;
Thy heart is strong, and the loud loom to-day
Stands where of eld thy skull-crowned ramparts stood
And Commerce in thy streets in peaceful mood
Pursues its hopeful customs now secure
Of loss of property and loss of peace :
And more than these—firm root of thine increase,
The blessing of thy people rich and poor—
Fair Knowledge reigns in thee, her rest and ease
Spreading from gate to gate, from door to door.
Thy sons have led her banners, first again,
In deeds of valour and of bravery,
The same in spirit as those stalwart men
Who here of old still held their own in thee ;
And she, fair Knowledge, honouring their zeal,
Has led them on to vie with cities great :
Thy Exhibition, equal to the hour,
Proving by its fair circumstance and state,
That for thy honour and thy people's weal,
Thou still hast hearts to strive, to pray, to wait,
Firm hearts, most strong where love alone is power.

   O "merrie city" of the ancient past,
City of pleasant scenes and old renown,
How sweetly art thou compassed !   Here at last
The tired wayfarer may at last sit down,
All Cumbria in his heart, and see again
All the fair scenes of this fair Border land :
Skiddaw and Criffel and Helvellyn's steeps—
Thy southern ramparts, one long mountain band,
Enlaced all round from their dark sombrous deeps
With tree-sloped vale and stream-engirdled glen,
A flower clad, brightening vista, on each hand.

Here too the silver Solway from thy heights,
Soft mantling on the distance, may be seen;
And Scotland's purple hills—long misty flights,
Where oft of yore her brave ones' feet have been,
Or where her bards have dwelt, their sounds and sights
The joy that blest them, kept their souls serene;
And nearer, fell on fell around thee creeps,
Their dark brows steeping in the radiant blue
Of the sweet summer; or when winter keeps
His storm-clouds marshalled, looking grandly through
The silver braiding of their swelling sweeps,
Half lost in its pale glory, but still true
To their stern form and features, better seen
When those dark clouds have fall'n, and the pale snow
Rests on their rugged shoulders, its pure sheen
Gracing their grandeur, the fair marble show,
The soul from far of the rude wintry scene
Of this north country, while the dark months flow.
And nearer still, still ready for the feet
Of wearied artizan, or o'ertasked child,
Or raptured lovers, bringing sweet to sweet,
Thou hast thy beauteous walks and scenes more mild;
The "Scaur," athwart whose heights the Romans piled
Their masonry enduring, the grand Wall
Which kept the Pict abeyant, o'er which frowned
The Roman legions, ready one and all,
From east to west, to keep this ancient bound
From foot incursive, where'er foot might fall.
Hard by where Hyssop Holme's green mantled steeps
Crown the famed "Well," most honoured of thy haunts,
This fabric ponderous paced the Eden's deeps,
Flying far on to where the Solway chants

Its monologue eternal, its bright bars
The terminus of this stupendous work,
Which here stood vast and awful 'neath the stars;
A splendid structure! which nor spear nor dirk,
But the strong hand of time at last threw down.
The tale in stone of these old nations' wars,
Of all the Roman works the head and crown.
This is a scene of beauty, soft and still,
Thy noises hushed by the prevenient space:
Thou liest across the river, street and mill
Behind the nobler features of thy face,
Thy fair cathedral and thy castle's tower—
From hence most fitly seen, its towering grace,
And massive ramparts, bringing back the hour
Of thy past triumphs, when this very place,
Loud with the artillery of war and death,
Flashed out their fearful flames, where now the flower
Gladdens the wanderer with its easeful breath.
O pleasant are these haunts, not less, but more
I love them for the past that here has been;
The life that ebbed out here in days of yore
Will keep these hills and vales for ever green
In human interest, brightening them all o'er
To days far distant, with the imagined scene
Of the great peaceless past, steeped to the core
In broils and turmoils, all its blazing sheen
Now dimmed and darkened, and its reeking roar
Silenced for ever by a hand serene.
    Tales are there many of this Border Land,
And of this Border city fair and free;
Tradition's subtle tongue, and time's dim hand,
Have woven about them things of mystery;

And in the winter, when the fire burns dim,
And garrulous guests have lost their wonted glee,
And the long night, far sloping to its rim,
Grows lone and awesome, mixing melancholy
With every breath, the peasant old and grey,
His heart fear palsied as his palsied limb,
Will tell, with the due meed of gaunt and grim
That makes a tale a tale—the flickering ray
And the weird silence all assisting him—
Such ghastly tragedies, that even fear
Itself exceeding, will itself o'erbrim,
Easing itself with the unbidden tear,
That at such times in listeners' eyes will swim.
But there are others of a softer frame,
Which deep in Cumbria's heart lie fast and sweet—
Tales of true love and trust and woman's name,
Which told, make winter hours as summer's fleet.
These are for female hearts and female tongues,
For household gatherings where the gentle meet—
Sweet ditties sweetly sung in Cumbria's songs,
With simple truth and trust and love replete ;
Tales unto which the virtue still belongs
To make the heart with genuine pleasure beat.
  So art thou girt about, strong on each hand
In Border lore and Border bravery ;
Thy sons, as any in this Border land,
Valiant and hopeful, resolute and free.
And in the coming time, the time of peace—
The time hope paints, which yet in truth shall be—
Their virtues firm, their scorn of fireside ease,
Their swift decision, and their energy
Shall be thy strength again, and thy old might

In every need shall still return to thee.
  Thy past has been a struggle stern and strong ;
The Danes of old turned their fierce fires on thee,
And thou laidst black and waste for centuries long,
A refuge but for want ; thy poverty
Bringing thee strange acquaintance ; and since then
Since Rufus raised thy walls of unknown date,
Raised long before by Rome, and yet again
By the good Egfrid, thou both soon and late
Hast oft been troubled, oft destroyed in part,
Thy fiery neighbour, the marauding Scot,
Still constant at thy gates ; but still thy lot
Has been to prosper ; and thy purer heart,
Strengthened by sorrow, unto virtue bound,
Nor undevoid of feelings which create
Religion's purer thought and purer life,
Shall still be thy protection, still thy state
Increase and prosper, and thy future strife
Enrich with nobler meed of nobler thought,
Bringing thee guerdon of things truly great—
A nobler spirit, and a wisdom fraught
With purposes diviner, of a reach
With the great coming ages, which shall teach
All men new doctrines, and shall all men free
With the pure power of purest Charity.

CARLISLE CASTLE.

THE FIRST ENGLISH PRISON OF MARY QUEEN OF SCOTS.

" How fair amid the depth of Summer green
Spread forth thy walls, Carlisle ! Thy castled heights
Abrupt and lofty : thy Cathedral dome
Majestic and alone ; thy beauteous bridge
Spanning the Eden, where the angler sits
Patient so long, and marks the browsing sheep
Like sprinkled snow amid the verdant vales.
Old Time hath hung upon thy misty walls
Legends of festal and of warlike deeds—
King Arthur's wassail cup ; the battle axe
Of the wild Danish sea-kings ; the fierce beak
Of Rome's victorious eagle : Pictish spear
And Scottish claymore in confusion mixed
With England's clothyard arrow.   Every helm
And dinted cuirass hath some stirring tale—
Yet here thou sitt'st as meekly innocent
As though thine eager lip had never quaffed
Hot streams of kindred blood.

Mrs. Lydia Sigourney.

IT is an old adage that familiarity breeds contempt ; and there is something of truth, but also something of untruth, in it ; for our contempt for what is familiar oftener arises from want of thought and reverence than from frequency of sight. "A thing of beauty," a thing of interest "is a joy for ever" to the refined, the intellectual, but like the famous potter, Peter Bell, of whom it is written that

> "A primrose on a river's brim,
> A yellow primrose was to him,
> And it was nothing more."

many of us in this old city of Carlisle are apt, we fear, to look upon our ancient castle simply as a castle, and nothing more ; either forgetful or uninformed of all its strange brave histories, and its equally strange and striking perils and pageantries and long silenced sorrows. In these days we read so much history that its *truth*—its vivid living realities almost escape us : we do not hear the rush and push and struggle of the brave, or see the tears and terrors which in far off homes, or subsequently, in nearer dungeons, were often their tragic accompaniment.

But coming out of the obliquity of the accustomed flow of house and street life, and standing as we stood on a bright November afternoon lately, in cells where the chained captive must often have sighed for death— thought returns, the imagination clears, and the wonderful panorama of the past rushes on and on before the excited mind in all the vivid hues of restless, changing, struggling, suffering human life. Sir Walter Scott said that "There are few cities in England which have been the scene of more momentous and more interesting events than Carlisle ;" and what is true of the city is true also of the castle, whose history is in reality the history of the city, and which has ample claim in comparison with all other castles in England to all that is stated in this assertion.

Carlisle Castle stands at the north west side of the city, on the left bank of the Eden, and is a massive building in the form of an irregular triangle, of various architecture, but principally in the Anglo Norman style, as the ingenious visitor will discern from its internal arrangement and construction, the material of its composition being chiefly red sand stone.

The entrance to it is through two ancient double gateways or towers of immense strength, and connect- ing the outer and inner wards, before both of which gates there was formerly a portcullis.

The castle now consists of one principal tower, with the ancient keep, (which is still in a sound and staunch looking state,) and the remains of what is called Queen Mary's Tower, from its having been the place where that unfortunate lady was confined in 1568, and which appears from its ornamental exterior to have been appropriated before that time to the use of royal or other stately visitors of the castle.

This tower is on the left side of entrance from the inner gate, and the interior of it is attained by going through the officers' rooms, including a large mess room, etc., which are at its rear, and which occupy the basement of what was formerly the chapel of the castle. But only a fraction of it is now standing, as its insecurity, it is said, necessitated its removal some years ago—a necessity much to be regretted by every intelligent visitor of the castle. Inside this tower, and in a sort of place which seems to have been extemporized into an officers' kitchen, there are still remaining a few of the steep steps of the stairs that once led up into it, and over which have doubtless rustled the floating trains of the beautiful quartette of Marys and their sorrowful mistress ; and we could not help thinking as we looked on them that the very foot which had taken precedence of the proud Catherine de Medeci in the regal ceremonials of courtly France, had passed in far different fashion up and down there.

A rampart of immense thickness and strength surrounds the castle on the north, east, and west sides, in which are embrasures for cannon. On the west side of this rampart is the present entrance to the tower, which opens into the armoury over the dungeons entered from the inner court. At present the arms in it consist only of about twenty very indifferent old swords hanging up and down on the bare walls, the interior of the room being occupied with a very goodly quantity of hospital clothing and requisites—and some of the rooms are filled with the general stores of the castle.

Leading out of these apartments, and on the same floor, are two cells which have been used formerly as places of confinement. One of them has the reputation of having been the prison of that eccentric Jacobite, Fergus Mc. Ivor, the hero of Waverley, and who, as the initiated know, was meant to represent the real, and we hope not less heroic, Major Mc. Donald of Kippoch. In this cell the loop hole looks out upon the pleasant Scotch country ; and on its base are two deep indentions of fingers, one of three, and the other of four, in what appears to be the solid stone. These are said to be the impression of the fingers of the poor Scotch prisoners, who as they incessantly stood gazing on their own dear distant hills, wore the impression of their strained fingers on the hard stone. It is a sad momento of the stern past, and one of the most pathetic of the many touching records time has left on these old walls. This cell has also an additional interest from the fact of Sir Walter Scott having been here on his last sad journey home—from Italy. He was accompanied by his daughter Ann, and the officious conductor, unknowing his visitor, explained to him how this had been Fergus's cell, and those the print of his fingers.

Outside these two cells there is a great deal of rude carving on the walls all around, of griffins, boars, scorpions, and armorial emblems, some of these latter being the arms of the ancient families of the county. There are some also of more pious design—women with lifted hands and eyes, and one with a child bearing the cross. One, too, we noticed, of Justice, her eyes bandaged, and the scales ; and there was one also of Fortune and her wheel. That grand monster of the good old times, the rack, is also duly depicted, as is its ally and competitor, the redoubted thumb-screw—figures under the operations of these mixing wofully with bands of pilgrims and solitary palmers, a pictorial compendium of the history of the times. These want no comment. Stolid indeed must he be who cannot read thoughts in things here ; and more stolid still who, when read, cannot sympathize with the great pondering, yearning human heart from which these thoughts flowed.

Passing from these cells, our conductor led us to an apartment on the same floor, containing a large quantity of exceedingly dusty lumber, among which he showed us what is said to have been Queen Mary's dining table. It is a veritable relic apparently, the two stands, one at each end, by which it is supported having been largely cut all round by the curious—not the reverentially—for chips or pieces of it. The table, which is a very plain, substantial one, is of oak, and about five feet in length by two and a half in breadth. Its antiquity is demonstrated by its workmanship, the nails by which the top is attached to the stands appearing in regular order on the surface of it. Poor Sir Francis Knollys, we fancy, if he had written that "story instead of a letter" he talked about, many a scene of it would have been described as taking place at this identical table. It was a sad charge his —sad for him, but still more sad for Mary. Here, during two long, sweet spring months, when the bright, glinting sun smiled down in beguiling blessedness over all the green rejoicing earth, peering even into her prison, with its old, old sweetness, how must that yet youthful heart have rankled under the unexpected restraint to which she was reduced. Often and often the substance of her thoughts must have been—

> Now blooms the lily by the bank,
>   The primrose down the brae,
> The hawthorn's budding in the glen,
>   And milkwhite is the slae ;
> The meanest hind in fair Scotland
>   May rove their sweets amang,
> But I, the queen of all Scotland,
>   Maun lie in prison strang.

There are tears, hot, burning tears, under those cere-
monious sentences she wrote to Elizabeth from here.
Her heart was full of them, though the Queen awed
the woman, and kept them there. Sad restless nights
must she have passed under those soft starry June
skies, though her days were pomped out with the regal
strain of her grand rank. It was the Queen who looked
on for two hours while her faithful followers played
football for her amusement "on a playing green towards Scotland," and that beautiful face undoubtedly
had its full complement of smiles and graces; but that
proud passioned heart in whose depths pulsed the
blood of the heaven-scaling Guises and the absolute
Tudors, must have had hours of dreadful hard human
suffering here, as it was here that her pleasant sustaining
dream of Elizabeth's sympathy and help was first so
utterly dispelled. But the heathery hills of Scotland
were still in sight here, and here also she could still hear
the clear ringing accent and heart hallowed speech of
her own loved land, and the attraction bound her— she
wished to stay here. Poor lady, on her beautiful head
descended the retribution of many wrongs. Queen of
Scotland, and born on its rugged soil, she yet through
her maternity and education was entirely French. All
her affinities with the Scotch nature had been destroyed,
and from this all her troubles sprang. She was the
victim of circumstances—the heiress of the results of a
century of mistakes and acrimonious unwisdom. We
must pity her. She must ever be pitied, and her final
treatment must be for ever deprecated. But still
Elizabeth acted not alone. Terrible things—the
Massacre of St. Bartholomew in 1572, in which at

least thirty thousand Protestants had been shamefully murdered, and the dreadful executions in the Netherlands by the ferocious Alva, of ten thousand Protestants, together with the sacking of Antwerp by the same Duke—had taken place during Mary's imprisonment, and these with the recollection of the fierce fires of Mary Tudor's reign, and the fear of their renewal, led the people as well as the nobles, who were already becoming ultra-Protestants or Puritans, to desire the death of Mary, who with Tudor tenacity still held fast to all the revoked ritual of her fallen church; thus allying herself with the enemies of England and her own country, and also with all the enemies of truth and progress and enlightend piety throughout the world.   Mary died a martyr to her religion, as she herself declared, when she took that last lone sacrament at Fotheringay; but it was the hard and fearful events of the times rather than the evil disposition of either the nobles or the people, or even the sovereign, which principally procured her death. *Requiescat in pace.* There seems injustice, but in the vast reaches of celestial jurisdiction good and evil interflow, and the wise and the thoughtful are reduced as they ponder the solemn mysteries of life and time to a devout belief in a sublime optimism, which for ever and ever, in large and in little, by suffering and by peace, works out a greater and still a greater good.

Concluding this episode, and taking a last look at this antique table, at which we almost seemed to feel the inspiring presence of the fair captive, we resume our explorations of the castle, our next progress being to the top of the tower, which is three stories high, each of sixteen feet in height, and which is, from the ground to the top of the parapet, sixty-eight feet in height. The prospect seen from here is a very fine one. On the south Skiddaw stretches its sublime circumference on the far off margin of vision, and to the west, beyond the silver Solway, rises the dark crest of Criffel, while the northern and eastern views are bounded by irregular heights of cloud capped fell, between which flows the tranquil Eden.

Within this area, and all around Carlisle, sweeps a beautiful and fertile extent of rich cultivated land, over which peaceful white villages and farms cluster thickly. This tract includes also many noted border towers and castles—Corby, Naworth, Brougham, Linstock, Penrith, and Rose Castle, for instance; but no helmed warders pace their keeps now. The times have changed, and one noble border chieftain, now, alas! no more, has sweetly tuned his peaceful lyre to the praises of the "wild and winsome jessamine tree" that blooms upon his border tower.

There are, also, many sweet rural solitudes in the interspaces of this prospect, where in the green summer time the honeysuckle and the wild rose and the satin-threaded bramble flower far up in mid air scatter their gracious healing beauty and fragrance on the unworldly wanderer. From here also the whole country may be reconnoitred for miles, the roads on every hand being visible for great distances.

Underneath the armoury, and on the ground floor of the tower are the solitary dungeons. They are entered mostly by narrow doors, and are utterly dark, no narrow chink of any kind communicating with the sweet upper air. The bare damp clay is all that is at the bottom of them, all round them at regular intervals are horizontal apertures, where we were told rings had once been to tie the prisoners up to, and the sad fact seemed but too conspicuously apparent for any less barbarous explanation. A large ancient gothic door in the inner ward, and not far from the inner gate, leads to these, from which there is a descent of stone steps, apparently the very same over which the bleached visages of those miserable prisoners must have come and gone. Grim, defiant faces, full of mad daring, and a wild half noble heroism, they rise upon the imagination; and what numbers of them must have passed that fearful threshold in the days when the slogan broke the bright silences of morning and evening full often round the purple hills of the border, and the hot-trod* was a common spectacle and a common fear to the irreclaimable moss-trooper. What numbers also must have repassed it to swift and summary execution, or in another fearful form as livid corpses, whose ghastly emaciations no bed had comforted, and whose last irrepressible sorrows no eye had watched, and no ear heard.

The outer and inner wards of the castle are separated by a wall and tower gate. The great tower, or keep, and the principal buildings of the castle, including those

---

* The hot-trod was a pursuit maintained with a lighted piece of turf carried on a spear with hue and cry, and bugle, horn, and blood-hound, and all who heard the alarm were expected to join in the chase. In many of the villages there were blood-hounds kept for this purpose.

we have seen, are in the inner ward, which is of a triangular form. Formerly this ward was enclosed by a wide and deep ditch, with a drawbridge; but there is scarcely a trace now of such having been. The tower gate is apparently of very ancient date, being all black and grim underneath, and bearing on its sides many quaint initials. On the left side of the entrance by this, there are still a great many ancient rooms and other buildings, some parts of which were taken down in 1820, and it was here that at that time the skeleton of a lady was found walled up. Looking up, on passing under the gate on that side, the place is still visible where this singular discovery was made, though the walls which enclosed it are gone. This lady, it is authentically stated, wore a Scotch tartan silk dress, and had on her fingers two gold rings, while her feet were placed on several silk handkerchiefs—facts which the curious may like to know, but which, nevertheless, avail little. There have been many conjectures respecting this mysterious person; and it has been made the subject of more than one tale; but there is no authentic idea, either traditional or otherwise, relating to it. The tales which have been written on it refer the atrocity of the deed to Richard, Duke of Gloucester, who was Governor of the Castle and Sheriff of Cumberland during his brother Edward the Fourth's reign; but this is entirely supposititious and quite questionable, as a wall built in the thorough fashion of those times at that date would scarcely have become insecure so soon as 1820. Nothing certain is, or can be known about this mystery. In the far past such dreadful deeds were not uncommon in many countries of Europe, and this may have been done by some impoverished Crusader, who, among his many ideas derived from travel and foreign association, had got this one of walling up alive any one whom jealousy or fear or avarice might make it desirable for him to dispense with. Ah! those were barbarous times, we exclaim. Truly, they were. Nor is the world quite free from that barbarism yet, nor will be till ambition, the great master passion of man, true to the central fact of all truth, revolves universally in its own legitimate track round Life, making that, in lieu of wealth, power, or position, the passion and purpose of existence.

Where all is so vague and conjectural, very little can be said; but in perambulating the precincts of the Castle it is well to pause here and let the mind realise the fact that a living lady was once the sufferer of an extraordinary barbarism there, since it is the spirit which we bring to or find amongst things which is the best help to knowledge, and which avails the most also in producing within us the faculties which lead to its proper use.

Passing out of this ancient gateway, before which now lies a very large open space of ground used for drilling, &c., and beyond which are the barracks, we come to the guard house and outer gate. The first of these is a very old place, close by the gate, with windows in the old barbaric style of one pane only. Our conductor told us there was nothing to be seen there, and so we did not go in; but these guard houses were the old novelist's favourite places for intrigues and midnight machinations; and could the old dim walls of this guard house articulate, we might possibly hear stories to fill and thrill the heart and haunt the imagination for many a day.

The outer gate is a lofty stone entrance of immense strength and thickness, and dim and black hued by time to a still greater extent than the inner one. It has also a greater number still of antiquated initials, and over it, on the outer side, is a defaced tablet of the arms of Henry the Seventh. This gate, from its appearance, must have been coeval with the most ancient parts of the castle, and, as such, is of great interest, as under its solid masonry must have passed and repassed all the notabilia of the castle from Rufus's reign downwards. Peaceful to-day as a mountain cotter's rose-garnitured threshold, it has other and different memories. Royal retinues, and princely and priestly pageantries and personages have passed under its awed shade, with curious or abstracted vision, and from its defied heights have issued the solemn cortege of pinioned prisoners for Gallows Hill. It has strange histories, if we knew them, that old outer gate. From 1122, when the courtly and learned Beauclerc was here, and most probably lodged in some prepared part of the castle, its walls have echoed with stately steps, and renowned visitors. Here—and very familiar with this place, having taken the city in 1135, and retreated here from the dreadful Battle of the Standard passed David, King of Scotland, for the last of many times, to die alone in his chamber, devoutly kneeling to the King of Kings ; and three years before that sad event, in 1150, our own Henry Plantagenet, then a ruddy, handsome, graceful youth passed here on his way, in company with the Earl of Chester, to this very

David, for counsel as to his course with Stephen. It ended in their entering into a league against Stephen, and Henry being knighted by David; and with such results, Henry most probably repaced this portal in pleasant spirits, the Earl of Chester and many a noble English youth by his side.

After David's death the castle again came into the hands of the English, and, twenty years after, we find that gallant governor, Robert de Vaux, pacing these old arches. A right heroic princely man, he rises upon us through the mists of time, his successful defence of the castle against William the Lion, of Scotland, during many months' siege, being the grand deed about which his name and fame revolve. And this was no common deed, for the city during that time was invested with 8,000 Scotch soldiers, and the resolute garrison were at fearful extremities, and on the very brink of yielding, when an accident—the Scotch king being taken prisoner at Alnwick—at last delivered them from their peril. Thirteen years after this Henry Plantagenet, now Henry II., again passed these portals. He was now no longer young, had reigned thirty-two years, and was within three of his death. Fierce struggles and fierce sorrows had passed over him, but great events and great things had also transpired and been done. Active, and hurrying hither and thither to the last, he came this time with a large army and met William the Lion (who had been in league with his own sons against him, but it seems forgiven,) and David his brother here. He was now lord of Scotland, William, on his defeat at Alnwick, having acknowledged himself his vassal; and the great king must have caused on this last visit of his a great deal of running and riding through this grand old gateway.

In 1216 another Scotch King appears on the scene —Alexander, successor to William the Lion. In this year that king took the city, after a long and miserable siege, gracing, undoubtedly, these dim walls with his daily presence for some short time. But his sway here was but of one year's duration, for, though England was in a troublous state then—the first year of Henry III. the English won back the city in 1213, and Walter de Grey, Archbishop of York, was made Governor of the Castle.

But the century did not close over the city and castle peaceably, for in 1296 siege was again laid to the city by the Scotch, though ineffectually this time, owing to the bravery of the inhabitants—the women even pouring boiling water over their heads from the walls, so that in three days it was abandoned by them. Stirring times these for these old walls, shrill women's voices even mingling with the martial din constantly pervading here !

At this very time—Scotland's fiercest foe, the fiery Edward the First, was pouring thousands of soldiers into the Border country, Dunbar and Falkirk battles being fought in 1296 and 1298, in which year the victorious Edward having reigned twenty-six years, and being at the height of his fame—marched his army here on their way from Falkirk ; and in the September following, while the white autumn mists silvered field and fell in the holy hours of twilight, winning to ecstatic contemplations and devotions, unknown, but not unhonoured saints, this ambitious king held a parliament within these walls.

A year before this Wallace himself had appeared before these walls demanding the surrender of the city, but once more we find the old city awake and vigilant in all needful dues for its own defence, and the brave Wallace himself retired from before it.

In 1300 Edward was again here on his route to Scotland, attended by his nobles and his army; and again in 1306, the very year his grand adversary, Robert Bruce, was crowned king of Scotland, and one year after the noble Wallace had been "hung, drawn, and quartered," most likely in his august presence, in his English capital.

This last time Carlisle was the appointed rendezvous of his army; and he himself was accompanied by his second young queen, Margaret of France, and his son Edward, Prince of Wales, eighteen years old that year. Here also, at the same time, were assembled nineteen bishops, and between fifty and sixty mitred abbots, the archbishop of York, and a great number of barons, with the Cardinal d'Espagnol, the Pope's legate. The redoubtable John Hilton, Bishop of Carlisle was at that time governor of the castle and factotum of the king in this border country, and during his stay here Edward was a frequent guest at Linstock castle, the Bishop's residence. All the succeeding winter of this year, and till the July of the following, the time of his death, the king and court remained either here or at Lanercost, and another Parliament was held here on the 20th of January, 1307. This was in all probability the acme of the great days of our castle—the grandest and most distinguished times these old Gothic walls ever knew. What gay hunting cavalcades, alight with sweet ladies' faces, their smiles and voices the wonder of northern ears and eyes, must have issued from these gates in the golden dawns of those years to Inglewood or otherwhere. And what great fires must have roared, that holy Christmas time, on the open hearths of the royal tower and apartments of this comely castle—a king and queen eating their brawn and plumb porridge in its then glowing chambers.

But these men, with all their faults, were something more than mere pleasure takers. War was their religion, and to its heroisms they devoted themselves, kindling the defiance they sought to subdue. They had conquered Wallace, one of the noblest patriots that ever breathed the sweet airs of earth, and of kindred, if not equal virtue, with Themistocles and the Gracchi; but he also had conquered them, and though now no more, his spirit survived in Bruce and his countrymen. It was in fact a Titanic war, great men being in both camps; but all our sympathies are with the brave Wallace and his brave compeers.

One little fact looming out here will show the superstitious tendency of even the strongest minds of that period. In the February of that year, 1307, Edward being already an invalid at Lanercost, and doubtless much mortified by the fact of Bruce's accession, despite of himself, to the Scotch throne, caused him to be excommunicated with bell, book, and candle, in the cathedral here, the Pope having previously commissioned the Archbishop of York and the

Bishop of Carlisle, the doughty John Hilton, to do this deed.

Among the governors of the castle sometime during the early part of this reign was John Baliol, the "Toom Tabard" of the Scots. He invaded Cumberland while king, and most probably gained some short space of sway here as a result. Bruce also was here more than once—the Bruce whose heart the brave Douglas carried forth to Palestine, though he never got there for his many wars. He was a hero of the grand line, and is one of the greatest presences that have graced these gates.

In 1307, after Edward II. had been proclaimed king in this city, on his father's death, and gone with all his "dool" vested followers to London, and from thence to France, to fetch his unfortunate "fate" Isabella, we find the same Robert Bruce besieging the city for ten days; but it was gallantly defended by Andrew de Harcla, the first Earl of Carlisle. In 1315 Bruce again besieged the place unsuccessfully, and eight years afterwards Harcla was arrested in this castle for having treasonously purposed to convert it into a garrison for his former enemy, de Brus. It is also said that that witty unprincipled favourite of Edward's, Piers Gravestone, was sometime governor of this castle, but if so, it must have been for a very short time. Let him pass. He is grand jester in our train of notabilia, and during his brief sway, if ever he ruled here, kept the old city company in its renowned characteristic right heartily we opine.

A quarter of a century after this, in 1335, we find the active and ambitious Edward III. here with a large army, his object being the assistance of his ignoble vassal, Robert Baliol, in whose interest he had two years before been at Hallidon Hill. Edward was little more than twenty-three when here, though he had already reigned eight years; but his head was already teeming with great ideas, and though we cannot sympathize with his mission, it must have been a sight worth seeing to have looked on that absorbed visage, as with his great ambitions just budding into determinate deeds—a real man under the gay garniture of person that then prevailed, he rode up and down this antique entrance. His five year old son, the Black Prince, with the good and wise Phillipa, his mother, was then at Windsor, a place which that great man, William of Wykeham, then but eleven years old, was soon to fashion into its present grandeur.

Bolingbroke and his sad captive, Richard II., are also said to have lodged here for a night on their way southward. A king in name and a real king: the man whom everybody blessed and the king whom nobody blessed—the melancholy, misled Richard, and the smiling, gracious Henry. Curious citizens would doubtless watch for these as they quitted at early morn these grey arches, looking with strained eyes after the royal cortege, while they brought up old memories and recounted new tales of the two principal figures in it. Poor Richard! the saddest king undoubtedly that ever passed out here; his sad downcast face mingles with the old vivid fancies of the castle as a pathetic phantom or a sorrowful apparition sent to touch the soft airs and fair stars of to-day with a sense of pity which now, as ever, makes the heart, amid all its vain ambitions, wise and good.

Ten years after Edward the Third's visit here, the Scotch again besieged Carlisle, burning both it and Penrith, and plundering very heavily, as it seems from the old chronicles. But once more they were defeated by the brave natives, their leader, the renowned Sir William Douglas, being taken and laid in irons in the castle, the common fate of all prisoners in those "stern old times."

We find also that during the Wars of the Roses, Carlisle was harassed to an unprecedented extent, and doubtless, the castle all through these Wars was the scene of strange and fearful events if we knew them. The scots especially sympathized with Henry the Sixth, and made an ineffectual attempt to take Carlisle for him ; and all through the reigns of Henry IV., V., and VI., the city was miserably harassed, the suburbs and adjacent parts, up to the very gates, being destroyed by fire. For all England this was a time of terror, and probably this old castle suffered greatly from the constant hostilities of the times, and doubtless many brave men and true passed these portals during all these years, for calamity also produces "thoughts that do often lie too deep for tears ;" and where we stand to-day as mere conjecturers, souls, whose names have been blown by heavenly trumps, may have prayed and perished, or, in the pressure of troubles, conceived thoughts or done deeds whose praise lingered in the local heart with loving pride for many a meagre-lettered generation.

Passing on to Edward the Fourth's reign, we find his brother, the notorious Duke of Gloucester, governor of the castle. He was also sheriff of the county, and must have been in the north for a considerable time, since we find him residing at Penrith Castle, then barely finished; and Camden says "this castle" i.e. Carlisle, "King Richard III., as appears by his arms, repaired;" and these repairs were most probably either planned or begun while Richard was here. There is also a tower called the "Tile Tower," or "King Richard's Tower," which was built at the same time. This Tile Tower is a very short distance west of the castle, and was originally on the city walls, being built to defend the wall on that side of the city. It is not a place of very large dimensions or height. One apartment only is open now, but out of this a doorway which led to some other has been walled up. A subterranean passage from the castle to the cathedral ran through the tower, and is said to have been used by Queen Mary and her ladies, but it is now walled up within on each side of the base of the tower, and the entrance to it, which was somewhere by the inner gate, has been closed up also. This building, which is now in a very dilapidated condition, bears the arms of Richard on its western side. We confess to being not very greatly interested in this king, yet though "cheated of feature by dissembling nature," he seems not to have wanted many of the principal characteristics of the Plantagenets, viz—strength, ambition, and resolution, and the genius of improvement; and his faults have in all probability been greatly exaggerated by our great poet, who doubtless remembered that the fair lady he wished to please was a Tudor. But if Richard himself is something lacking in interest, the time of his stay here was one of particular note in the

history of modern times, for during that time William
Caxton was revising his first proofs in the sacred
purlieus of Westminster, and Christopher Columbus
was waiting on the western coast of Spain in a poor
convent for the means to realize his sublime idea of a
vast India over the virgin waves of the great Atlantic.
Both these things perhaps were in Richard's thoughts
as he came and went here, and not improbably formed
the topic of talk at some of the suppers he and his
retainers ate together in our castle.

After this, and in 1537, we find, as a result of the
growing intelligence of the times, the first signs of
desires for peace between the English and the Scots.
In that year, and most likely within the walls of the
castle, the Bishops of Durham and Orkney met at
Carlisle as commissioners for a treaty of peace between
the two countries. But these ancient towers had
many a storm in reserve then, the first of which
occurred in the very same year—the year of the Pil-
grimage of Grace. In that year the city was besieged
by those misguided men, which resulted in their being
repulsed by the garrison and citizens, and seventy-four
of their principal officers being executed on the city
walls. Subsequently, their ghastly heads gleamed
from these towers or the walls, scaring the mid-day
airs even with fearful terror; for these were not the
hated Scotch, but English gentlemen, and some of
them probably well known and much loved in the city.
There must have been many a sad procession through
these gates, both in and out, during this "rising."
Here in these border counties the two great antagonistic
forces of the time, Protestantism and Catholicism,

met, and the latter was utterly defeated. It was too late to burn Bibles as they were burnt by the people at Durham ; too late to restore the mass in England, though for a century after this hope lingered in the Catholic heart ; still, the genuine enthusiasm of many of the leaders of this Rebellion, gives a touch of grandeur to the determinate effort of this desperate band of men, and adds to the regret which spontaneously rises in generous minds in contemplating the fearful severities they suffered. One in every village for sixty miles around, and in many of them many more, was hung, to awe the disaffected. It was a sad time. Anti-progressionists have ever been persistent persecutors, and most of all so in all times when the progression has been one in connection with Religion—the mind of man still confounding its passing forms with its eternal spirit and substance. In the year 1400, a century and a quarter before this, the stake had been set up in England, but the flame only increased the fury of zealots, the unswerving victims of the inquisition, by their noble behaviour, but creating new supplies for its horrid tortures ; and in conjunction with this the grim age still held its cord and axe. as though sure of the occasion which, in the insecurity of the times, was never wanting. It was the God of the Old Testament, not of the New, the age worshipped—a God of vengeance, not the God of Love ; and Shakespeare, yet unborn, had yet to teach men the qualities of mercy, and how

"It becomes
The throned monarch better than his crown."

In 1596 we find that famous borderer, Kinmont

Willie, in irons in the castle. He was taken prisoner during a time of truce, and imprisoned contrary to the express agreement of the truce, and William Scott, the Lord of Buccleuch, whose follower he was, demanded his instant release. This demand was not complied with, and his angry chief, after the fashion of those times, came here at once with two hundred horsemen, provided with ladders for scaling the walls, and instruments of iron for forcing the gates; and before the garrison could prepare for resistance, in the brightening dawn of an April morning, forced the castle, and carried off the renowned Willie, his irons still on, which Sir Walter Scott says a smith knocked off at a cottage by the road side between Longtown and Langholm. Summary proceedings these. These men had not yet acquired our modern notion of debating the question. They did not palter whatever they did, nor cheat their consciences with the questionable virtue of votes.

Another of our English monarchs, James the First, visited Carlisle in 1617, and very probably lodged in the castle, perhaps in the very apartments his mother once occupied. The object of his journey to Scotland —the establishment of Episcopacy in the place of Presbyterianism— was a very unwise one, and together with his intolerance of the English Puritans and his universal despotism, the source of all the long train of evils that troubled all, or nearly all, his descendants. But the pedant king appears to have found favour with the pleasant people of Carlisle, for they, with all due speechifying and kissing of hands, presented him with a "cup of golde" valued at thirty pounds, and "a

purse of sylke containing forty jacobuses of the same."
A most welcome gift we have no doubt to the needy
monarch, who, we are told, used this obliging " Maiore
and his brethren very gracceouslye."

At this time James had been fourteen years in
England, and was more than fifty years old. His
eldest son and heir, Henry, was already dead in his
prime, his Queen, Ann of Denmark, was a trouble to
him, and the country was fermenting with the new
religio political emotion of Puritanism, made daily
stronger by his prohibitions. Three years after this
the May Flower left the coast of Holland for America;
and while James was here receiving cups and purses
of gold from the gracious Mayor and citizens, many
of the noblest of his subjects were flying from his
arbitrary rule to Holland and other places, and the
great men who were to put the disjointed times right
—Milton, Cromwell, and Hampden, were already
ripening into manly life and deed. But James was
no seer, and consequently, with "feast royall" and
public church going, enjoyed himself in right kingly
style here with his rattling retainers and the "merrie"
citizens, he and they talking Armenian Theology and
Universal Episcopacy in the calmer intervals of their
noisy plays and pageantries.

In 1639 five hundred Irish soldiers were sent as a
garrison to this castle, and remained here two years.
The commotion in Scotland caused by the imposition
of Bishops, etc., necessitated this precautionary move-
ment. The great struggle was just commencing
between king and people, which for more than ten
years after this was to break nearly every sweet silence

of wood and field between the Grampians and Land's-
end with the fierce din of war. And in this war this
city and castle had a full share of the general tumult
of the times. The royalists held the city in 1644, of
Marston Moor memory, and we find General Leslie
besieging Sir Thomas Glenham, commander-in-chief
for his majesty here the same year. More than seven
months this siege lasted—from October, 1644, to
June, 1645, a long winter through, and the calamity
consequent was very great. " Flesh of horses, dogs,
and other animals " was for some time the subsistance
of the besieged. The old city, notwithstanding its
bravery, must have been fearfully tried during all this
time, and gaunt anxious faces must have passed
through these old arches in those drear winter months;
but the brave garrison capitulated to Leslie at last,
almost death driven.

In 1648 the city again fell into the hands of the
Royalists, having been taken by surprise by Sir Philip
Musgrave, who after two months' occupation gave it
up to the Duke of Hamilton, and by him it was
garrisoned with Scots, Sir William Livingstone being
appointed governor. This same year, on the first of
October, and after the defeat of Hamilton and Lang-
dale at Preston, by Cromwell, this city also quietly
surrendered to him. During this year the city had
been the scene of the most distressing suffering. The
siege of Carlisle of 1644-5 is one of three of the most
determined for the king's cause. Isaac Tullie, who
was in the city the whole time, gives a very striking
account of it. " The citizens' clothes hung on them,"
he says, " like those of men on gibbets ; and one day

some officers and soldiers came to the common bake-
house, and took away the horse flesh from the poor
people who were as near starving as themselves.

"Women met at the cross abusing Sir Henry
Hadling the governor, who threatened to fire upon
them; they begged it as a mercy, and the old soldier
went away with tears in his eyes—he could not help
them. This was Leslie's siege." Sad troubled times
of change and commotion were these, but the strong
man had now come, and the storm subsided. Cromwell is one of the very noblest and bravest who have
graced these gates; and even to-day, dwelling on
those stormy times, his presence is half realized.
Fresh from the signal victory, or rather victories, at
Preston, his heart, as he passed these portals, which
he undoubtedly did, would perhaps be revolving his
favourite Scripture, "Why do the heathen rage, and
the people imagine a vain thing? The kings of the
earth set themselves, and the rulers take counsel
together against the Lord and against his anointed,
saying, 'Let us break their bands asunder and cast
away their cords from us. He that sitteth in the
heavens shall laugh, the Lord shall have them in
derision.'" Brave Oliver! we wonder if he also lodged
within these towers, and whether amid all the multi-
tude of sounds that have passed hence, the audible
morning and evening prayer of that great true man
mingled.

Pacing these arches on a different errand, another
great hero of the time was at this castle, in 1653.
This was that truly noble man, George Fox, whose
manly zeal inspired him with the idea of preaching to

the garrison here.   His discourse was most likely
delivered in the inner court of the castle, and it being
the fourth year of the Protectorate, it is not improbable
that some of Cromwell's soldiers might be intermixed
with the troops, which may account for his favourable
reception, for we find the soldiers on the morrow
taking his part when he was arrested after preaching
at the Market Cross.   However this may be, his being
here adds to the interest of these ancient walls, and to
him who lingers lovingly over all their great past, im-
bibing not only the fact, but the spirit of the times out
of which the fact grew, this one calm voice amid the
multitudinous din of years will be precious indeed—
precious as the augury of a new era, as the first
receding wave of a many centuried strife-tide which,
not here only, but throughout the whole world, had
spread perpetual desolation and perpetual sorrow.   It
would be worth much now to many to annihilate the
intervening years, and catch but for one brief minute
the look and tone that pierced the hearts of that
grotesque auditory on that special day in this castle
court.   So plain a man and yet so powerful, so
courageous and yet so humble he rises on the imagination ; and then his truth so great that it has yet to
live on and refresh unknown generations—not yet
fully apprehended, but finally to be both apprehended
and honoured.   No wonder that a preacher of such
doctrines—a denouncer of routine and formula—
should here, as every where, have found a prison.
One of the most faithful and farseeing of the spiritual-
ists of all times, his imagined presence still hallows
these scenes ; and though there is no authentic proof

of his having been confined in these dungeons, yet his followers, as well as others, may still gain some instruction by coming to see where he preached.

A century after this, in 1745, the "Young Pretender," Charles Edward Stuart, came hither from Scotland with an army of nine thousand men, and laid siege to the city on the 9th of November, demanding its instant surrender in the name of his father. On the 15th the gates of the city were opened to him, and his father was proclaimed king at the Cross. This done, they marched southward as far as Warwickshire, contemplating, in their hour of victory, the subduction of the metropolis. But other and sadder fortunes awaited them. The Duke of Cumberland was already in the field as their opponent, and at Derby they found three armies in front of them. Charles Edward, perhaps wisely for him, following the counsels of his officers, at once retreated before these forces, taking the direct way back to Carlisle, the Duke and his ponderous army all pursuing. The Prince's army arrived in Carlisle on the 19th of December, after some severe skirmishing at Penrith the previous day. The Duke followed hard after, and, in the interval of eleven days, Carlisle, with little loss, was once more in the hands of his majesty King George. During this interval the city had been besieged, the fire of the besiegers being directed "wholly against the Castle," which the Duke in scorn had called "a miserable hencoop," and which Lord Murray, of the Prince's army, would have blown up, if his own will had been done, ere the Prince's party left it. The castle was in fact the great scene of action during all this disastrous time.

Three hundred and ninety-six men, of various ranks, became prisoners of the Duke by the recapture of the city. Hamilton, governor of the castle, and Colonel Townley, governor of the city, were subsequently executed in London, undergoing to the letter, as did all the long list of these prisoners, their whole horrid sentence of being half hung, embowelled while yet alive, and afterwards quartered. The heads of Hamilton, and Cappoch, the "rebel bishop," were sent to Carlisle and placed on the Scotch gate, and the heads of Captain Berwick and Lieutenant Chadwick were also sent, and placed on the English gate.

The August following 382 prisoners were sent here, after the Battle of Culloden. Of these, 125, all heavily ironed, were thrust into *one room* in the castle keep—probably the large cell on the ground floor— partial suffocation and indescribable miseries assailing them while they awaited the tender mercies of judge and jury. Many of these were afterwards executed, numbers at Gallows Hill in the ensuing October and November, among whom was Major Mc.Donald of Kippoch, (the Fergus Mc.Ivor of *Waverley*,) a really brave and generous gentlemen, his head all beautiful with bonny bland locks "fearsomely" withering for long after on the Scotch Gate, he himself having, with his companions in sorrow, been hung, drawn, and quartered at the common place of execution, where now blooms the golden celandine encinctured with dappled daisies. Besides these, six were executed at Brampton, seven at Penrith, and twenty-two at. York. So ended these last efforts of the Stuarts. They were gallantly made, but they shared the sad fate of all their projects—the blood of many a strong Scotch heart being the unhappy result. There is much in Sir Walter Scott's *Waverley* illustrative of this special enterprise with which every visitor of the castle should be acquainted, as these old stones will be nothing to him whose heart has never been touched by the emotions of pity and regret for the noble young hearts that perished in their shadow.

Sir Waiter Scott himself is among our notabilia, having visited the castle many times—a reverend and loving connoisseur of all its old glories and many legends, "part seen, imagined part." How he lingered in these old stately ways with his soul o'erbrimmed with thought, we can well imagine every tower and turret bringing to his great worshipping heart some tale of that stirring past of his country and this brave Border land on which he so loved to dwell.

Besides him, it has been visited by many noble and learned authors; but it has no book for visitors' names, and, consequently, they are but very indefinitely known. Mrs. Sigourney of America is something of an exception to this rule, as she has immortalized her visit by her ready pen. As Mary Queen of Scots first English prison she seems to have visited it, and on the other side of the Atlantic its fame is almost exclusively derived from this sad circumstance.

We close the list of our notabilia with the present Prince of Wales. He visited the castle when about fourteen. It was a mere tourist's visit on his way to Scotland one bright summer morning; but we hope in time to come, when he has won the noble fame of a just and wise king, even this short visit may be remembered and added to the worthiest memories of this ancient castle.

The exact time of the erection of this castle is uncertain ; but it is supposed to occupy the site of the old Roman fort, which was probably one of those built by Agricola in his *westward* progress to Scotland, about the year 80. That it was originally of Roman construction is proved by a Roman well which still exists in the north wall of the keep, and which was made of an immense depth, for the purpose of furnishing the garrison with a supply of water which could not be cut off by an assailing enemy. Egfrid the Christian king of Northumbria, and a descendant of Bertha, the wife of Ethelbert, king of Kent, through their daughter Ethelburger, repaired the castle in 680 ; and six years after we find the Bishop of Lindisfarne at Carlisle to obtain an audience of Queen Ermengard, the wife of Egfrid, who was then on a visit to her sister, the abbess of the nunnery here. Egfrid, it is possible, was at the castle at the same time as the great Bishop is said to have been his guest; but whether or not, the citizens brought St. Cuthbert out to show him their walls and this famous well while he was here ; and as we stood in the very place where the holy man had stood so many dim centuries ago, and looked down its morticed sides, a cartoon of the whole scene involuntarily arose upon the imagination—the devout Christ-hearted Cuthbert, and the curious awed train of Volanti "people of the forest," as the inhabitants of these northern counties were then called, which undoubtedly followed him.

Two centuries after this the city was destroyed by

the Danes, the castle in all probability being greatly injured, for the whole place, it is said, lay in desolation for the space of two centuries, till in 1072 the Conqueror returning from Scotland, ordered the city to be restored and fortified. But it was not till 1092, when Rufus also returning from Scotland, observing the beautiful situation of the city, ordered it at once to be rebuilt; and this included the restoration of the castle, which forthwith proceeded without delay. Ranulph de Meschines, who before this time had received Cumberland as a grant from the Conqueror, was the restorer of Carlisle. He was a very noted man of those times, and one whose name is deeply inwoven into the past annals of this city and county.

Previous to this a few poor Irish alone tenanted the forlorn and devastated city; but about this time a colony of Flemings had settled here, it is said, for a while, being at length "replaced by a colony of south Britons, who cultivated the wild Forest of Inglewood, and taught the natives the art of profiting by the natural fertility of the soil." These in all probability —i.e. the Flemings and Britons—were the principal "hands" in raising once more the solid bastions of our ponderous castle. Let us pause a moment, and looking through the silent centuries, try to get a sight of those quaint, strange tongued men working in the same holy sun which shines to-day. How modern they are—they shout and joke and laugh as though they wore corduroy and ankle-jacks, and anon they praise the Red Roysterer for his sagacity in appreciating the fertile country and the precious worth of the old city, and also for his energy in action respecting it,

4

their poor animated Irish hodmen meanwhile per-
forming some equivalent for tossing their caps—for
caps there were none in those days—their prolix
tongues, then as now, always ready with a chorus for
every chant.   But where are all those brave workers
now?   They also are gone with all the brave thousands
who have defended or assailed these gates before or
since.   But we feel to-day that these also are sanctified
by death and time, and that their honourable names,
though unknown, are woven into the great anagram of
human helpers, and also into the notabilities of our
castle.

Before closing this sketch, there are one or two
things of interest which seem to demand some word
or two.   The first is respecting "The Lady's Walk,"
which lies on the outside of the outer Gate, the gate
called "John de Ireby," (the inner one for some unknown reason being called "The Captain.")   It leads
along close by the outer wall on that side till it comes
to a postern now walled up, which formerly led to the
Sorceries, and through which Queen Mary and her
ladies would pass when they went to see the football
playing on "a green toward Scotland."   This postern
may still be seen by persons going the usual way to
what is called the "Castle Bank."   The door from the
castle to this walk has also been walled up, but may
be recognised by a shield charged with the arms of the
Dacres over it.   Formerly two ash trees, planted,
tradition says, by the captive Queen, grew here,
forming an ornamental appendage to the castle.   They
were cut down in 1804, by order of the Board of
Ordnance, a proceeding as little to be understood as
commended.

On the outer wall of the ancient Chapel of the castle, close behind Queen Mary's Tower, and which seems from its architecture to have been of Tudor origin, are the arms of Queen Elizabeth, with an inscription to this effect—" Queen Elizabeth made this work at her own expense, while Lord Scrope was Warden of the Western Marches." It was originally on the old barracks, and the work in question was most likely "made" about the time that this Lady, siding with Mary in her fallen fortunes, against the Lords, charged this Lord Scrope to allow the Scotch marauders of the Borders to pursue their course unmolested, Bothwell's followers being supposed to be among them. Opposite to this Chapel, which the visitor will easily recognise, the ramparts are all hollow, having a face of stone to the inner ward in the building, of which the curious may see several stones, which still bear the diamond shaped mark of the Roman pick on their exterior, proving them to be nearly eighteen centuries old, the remains, most likely, of some more ancient and ruined part of the castle, which is now entirely non-existent. At the end of this, and by Queen Mary's Tower, there are also the remains of an ancient portcullis, the use of which seems now somewhat inexplicable, but in the olden days of the castle it doubtless had one.

In the cells also let the visitor look carefully at the locks ; some of them are now detached and hanging in the armoury. Each door had four, and their weight and size is something extraordinary, some of them being of themselves a good half-hundredweight. But cumbrous and heavy as they are they will still act—

the bolt still flying in response to the ponderous key, though in all probability some of them are more than a thousand years old.

In the upper rooms of the keep the visitor may also see remains of the ancient spiral stairs which led to the top, and with which there seem to have been private communications in different places. He will notice also that the immense rooms at the top have had a door between them, in the centre of the wall, which is now closed up, and that opposite to this closed up door, is a fire place, also closed up. Probably in these large rooms the Parliaments were held which have been held here; and it is not impossible to imagine that the large courts occasionally remaining here may have been feasted, and perhaps some of their numbers even bedded in these spacious chambers now, happily for the times, entirely silent, and divest of all their former martial adjustments, their strange and changing histories almost wholly conjectural. Yet we know that hearts with human passions once beat here, and that forms now dead and turned to clay once animated this forlorn silence.

There are many other traditions of the castle than these. It is said, for instance, that King Arthur and his renowned knights once drank their wassail bowl within it; and hence the story of King Arthur's cup, which tradition is doubtless truth. There are many traditions, too, of Lord William Howard, the "Belted Will" of Border story; but truth and fiction are so largely blended, that to dissever and disentangle is almost impossible. This gentleman was, it is true, the Warden of the Marches here for many years, and was doubtless a frequent visitor of the castle, his vigour in putting down the mosstroopers being a special advantage to the city, which before his time was constantly suffering from their depredations. He was in reality a good and worthy man, possessing even in the midst of his stern work, many of the fine tastes of his renowned ancestor, Sir Philip Sidney; he himself, as my reader should note, being a son of that Duke of Norfolk who lost his life for his tender attachment to Mary Queen of Scots.

Whatever we have missed of all the scenes and story of this really interesting relic of antiquity, we feel that for our purpose it is enough to know that here is a spot which, for nearly eighteen lasting centuries of night and day has really been the focus of a great share of all the events and histories of our brave England; and that where we stand to-day, many of all the bravest and noblest men of those centuries have stood also. This we know is true, and hence the inspiration and instruction these many-centuried walls afford. The shout of warders and guards is all silent now; but those old ages have left stern witnesses of their strength in these twelve feet thick walls; and these are at the same time witnesses also of the persistent courage and practical wisdom of the antagonists of this city. The castle is in fact a condensed history of the past—of all the jealousies and criminal ambitions of rival nations, and all the evils and miseries which spring from unchristianized might; and its dim walls and dark dungeons, with their now darkened grating, to which sad hungering eyes once looked so anxiously and enviously, coveting the blessed light, with all the other saddening purlieus of the place, still, well repay the visitor who values either poetical emotion or suggestive and enlarging thought.

CORBY CASTLE AND WALKS.

N the race days at Carlisle, which occur shortly after Midsummer, a great number of Excursions are generally made to the most beautiful or noted parts of the county. Issuing out with a large party with one of these, we, with many pleasant friends, left the flushed, bustling, far-travelled throng of our usually sober city, for Corby. The morning had been showery and unpromising, but at noon—our hour of starting—the clouds cleared off, and from the clear blue of the open sky, fell the full, far-sweeping rays of the gladdening glorious sun. Under its pure beautifying glory we started on our way, the rich scythe-waiting meadows, the densely-foliaged trees, and the sheets of fresh and apparently fadeless flowers beneath them, and stretching their long trails into every nook of nature, giving the first taste of that hallowing joy which nature never fails to give to those who love her. So passing Durran Hill Cottage, the clean, quiet, well-to-do village of Scotby, and the pretty new Station at Wetheral, we came to Corby Bridge, where we alighted. Right on we passed through the village, clean and trim and bright with roses and carnations—which spread

their splendid hues before and behind the quiet cottages till we came to the lodge gate—the lodge, which
is a very worthy appendant of the castle, being our
first object of admiration.   Here all at once the scene
of beauty opens.   There is only a very short distance
between this and the castle, which, in a few steps,
reveals its square substantial outline, brightened on
its eastern side by the rich profuse bloom of the showy
rhododendron, and a glass conservatory, full of choice
and beautiful flowers, the rich varieties of geraniums,
calceolarias, and balsams being now at the very acme
of their brilliance.   The castle itself has no castleated
roof, nor any of the usual features of the real Gothic
castle, but is a large handsome massive structure, in
the modern style of architecture, surmounted by a
well-executed collosal lion, which gives an air of
princely beauty to the whole building.   Fronting the
castle is a fine flowing lawn, which gently descending
effectively sets off its stately proportions, and being
plain, is in excellent keeping with them.   The castle
contains several fine pictures—one by Titian—and
several curious and interesting antiquarian relics.

But the Walks are the great object of interest, their
unprecedented beauty, causing, it is said, even Hume
to break out into verse when he visited Carlisle, where
he left traced on the window of his hotel—

> " Here chicks in eggs for breakfast sprawl
> Here godless boys God's glories squall,
> But Corby Walks *alone for all.*"

Leaving the castle on the right, we proceed to the
walks close at hand.   These consist of many acres of

land, densely wooded, rocky, precipitous, sloping down
to the Eden, on whose banks they lie, in some places
by abrupt perpendicular declivities, in others by cir-
cuitous paths, under a canopy of interlacing branches,
impervious to the most penetrating rains, and also to
all the sunshine of the year, however piercing, however
radiant. Many noble trees of all kinds are here, and
one old trunk deserves especial notice, on account of
its immense size and poetic appearance, being hollow
at the bottom and "wreathed and crowned" with ivy
at the top and round its sides. How many thoughts
that old tree suggested of our ancient England, and
the wild wildering years fraught with the exhalations
and voices, the breath and bruit of persons and things
now become almost, or quite questionable, from their
very remoteness, or perhaps lost entirely from the great
roll of the world's accredited and accepted facts.
What was our England when this tree was a seedling
or a sapling? Over what cradles were Englishwomen
singing their strangely-lettered lullabies? or what was
the staple masculine discussion at the castle dinner, or
in the scriptorium amongst the shaven monks, who
were making the margins of their manuscripts bright
with the floral emblems of the names of their sainted
loves? Something of this might perhaps be acquired
by learning the exact age of the tree—but, oh! how
little and uncertain.* That world with all its woes
and wonders has passed away, leaving us but the dead
ashes of what was once its living substance—a form-

---

* Since the above was written, Mr. Howard himself informed
the present writer that this venerable tree was eight hundred
years old.

less, dissimilar, disproportionate residuum, from which
scarcely one element, or one true outline of the
genuine feature of the life and knowledge that then
were can be traced. With these thoughts, and many
inexpressible ones, we turn from that old tree, feeling
that

"There is a spirit in the pathless woods,"

and feeling also some sympathy with those old, old
worshippers who found in trees and rivers the mystery
and awfulness out of which they wove the garment of
God—their grand, yet heartless God, of force of
power.

All ways we look as we pass under these stately,
solemn denizens of memorial and immemorial time,
fearing lest we lose any of the imposing, soul-abstracting
beauty they so abundantly display, our hearts o'er-
brimming, although we have but just entered, with
feelings which, like odoriferous incense, carry us away
to the vast, the illimitable, to the heaven of an enlarged
existence, far above and beyond the fret and fever of
all our petty cares, and still pettier ambitions. Gliding
on, for we walk as in a church, through these solemn
aisles of prototypal ecclesiastical architecture, we come
to the well—the Wishing Well we are told—whose
cool crystal waters, together with the kindly placed
cups, are an irresistable temptation to the summer
wanderer. Nor did the majority of our party forget
the Wishing business, which is done mentally before
drinking—the taciturn bearing of the whole party of
them respecting their wish causing much merriment.
The Well itself is a cistern placed against the des-

cending earth or rocks, into which the spring runs, and which is surmounted by solid masonry, upon the front of which the saintly symbol of human help is placed.

Speedily, for we are on a descending path, we come to an opening, and turn around to the left to seek the recollected hermitage, a little round, cross-surmounted mosshouse, where used to sit in state with girdle and sandals, the bearded hermit, holding the long-stringed numeral of his many prayers. There was no hermit, but the recollection to ourselves, and the description to others, seemed to suffice very well for his absence.

Leaving this, and going back and onward, we come to a long straight open avenue, a sort of long shelving table land between the upper and lower declivities. Here again are the beautiful green sward and the sunshine, the latter heightened by the dark dominant dome of foliage, it winningly but vainly woos to dissipation. At the far end of this, in our front, is the beautiful Summer House, or "Temple D' Ete'," so well known, which is a beautiful sylvan structure, ascended by a long flight of steps, and having a balcony on the right side, under which bloom intertwined with the deeper green of the fir, fair flowery shrubs—eyes through which nature seems to look dispassionately and saintly as a musing seraph. Inside there are pictures, and all the necessary requisites for repose or meditation, the different panels of the room being pictured with foreign scenes and scenery, and the ceiling with an eagle and a fish, while smaller birds are enviously or fearfully winging around. The day being rather dubious, a fire had been very thoughtfully and kindly lighted for us, by the order, doubtless, of the noble and generous master of the place. Descending from the steps of this Summer House, the splendid avenue leading from them shows all its many beauties It is indeed a matchless strip of green earth, noble under all aspects, and in all seasons. At various distances through its length, seats are placed for the repose of the weary, attached to which are printed quotations from the poets for their delight and inspiration.

Under the balcony on the path which leads by the river, almost dark with thick umbrageous branches, we now take our way. Here Nature has her own will, and it is a sweet one, order in disorder, life many-formed and many-hued everywhere. And here is the river musical and magnificent. How pleasantly it unites its sweet symphonies with the sunshine and the breeze, and the fluttering, yet incessant quirings of the overhanging woods; and when these have all ceased,

"When thickest dark doth trance the sky,"

it will still harmonize. Nature never strikes the wrong note. The holy stars and the silent solemn earth will be to-night the wrapt auditors of this eternal wanderer —this awful orator whom time and death never disable, never still.

Returning from here, and down the avenue, we come to "the coups," where the sheeny waters of the river are broken into foam and fury; but under all forms the river here is grand and glorious—a real thing of beauty, making as it did ours, the heart dance with supremest joy. From this spot there is a beautiful view of the castle—perhaps the best view—its wooded environs which are here seen with it, adding their regal robing to its noble proportions, and enlarging to a graver, greater grandeur, its massive outline.

Later, we crossed the river, on the Wetheral side of which are the ruins of Wetheral Priory, founded for Monks of the Benedictine Order by the Earl Ranulph de Meschines, about the year 1086. A magnificent view of the Corby side of the river may be had from one of the top windows of this building, or from the caves, which are immediately below, on the same side. These are excavations in the solid mass of rock which rises almost perpendicularly on this side of the river. St. Constantine's cell is the most notable one. A Prince of this name, the son of some ancient Scottish king, is said to have resigned his regal inheritance and here retired from the world for the remainder of his life ; and opposite them, on the Corby side, those interested will find a representation of him in the habit of a monk, a cross and missal in his hands, and the earthly crown at his feet—all hieroglyphical of his life and deeds. The rocks on this side the river are very romantic and beautiful for a considerable distance, the abrupt heights being charmingly interspersed with wood.

It is said that these caves were for many centuries the shelter of the ancient inhabitants of Carlisle when their city was attacked by the Scots, or by their still fiercer and more remorseless enemies the mosstroopers, of whom they were in constant dread ; and the place must certainly have been a good one in those perilous times.

Being on the Wetheral side, we now took the opportunity of visiting the Church, which no one visiting Corby should omit doing, one of the divinest pieces of statuary, and by one of the very chiefest artists, Nollekins, being there. It is an emblematical memorial of the late Mrs. Howard, and said to be the artist's *chef d'œuvre.* Near it is another, by Flaxman, of the ordinary ecclesiastical type.

As we waited in the evening sun for the boat to take us back again, our hearts lifted and hushed by the grandeur of art, and thoughts of the vastness of the soul, and the splendours of its achieved and possible realizations, we seemed more fully cognizant than ever of the sweeping scene of beauty that stretched before us. Never shall we forget that sit on the stone by the river. We had been talking of the illustrious dead and noble living, and remembered fragments of thought and song had come home to our open spirits, and as we looked up and down the river and on its galleried sides, crowded with the lofty heads of the noblest trees, and these all flushed into a thousand changing lines by the descending sun, we felt the full intensity of Natures's holy hallowing power—felt that God has wealth for all ; that noble heart wealth of gladness in beauty, in Nature, and in art.

Again in the Walks, we followed on by winding paths to the caves on that side, whose surrounding beauty we should almost profane by attempting to describe. But the caves—the matchless masonry of Nature, hollows in the solid perpendicular rock, and opening on the river—how they silence all trivial thought, and make one forget flesh and blood.

"Thoughts that wander through eternity" start here, and we think of the sublime silences of unpeopled centuries which these sunken, lidless eyes in this ponderous rocky brow of nature must have seen the secrets of. Before the one furnished with pictures, seats, and table, there is a pallisading parallel with the river, and over this, when the sun is descending, if he can, let the visitor of Corby give himself time to hang and muse till he hears nothing, sees nothing, not even the faces and voices of his friends, but this everlasting pageant of natural harmony and vision. From the steps also of the other cave, in the perpetual twilight of depending branches, there is a magnificent view. But our friends have nearly all left us to our tranced speechless musings, and we, though loath, must on. One moment however we must have standing at the green pond by the somewhat dilapidated Nelson, to look up at the rocky heights dripping with ceaseless waters. It is a semicircle of rock shelving up to an immense height, on the top of which is a ruined fane, containing fragments of tritons and nymphs, whose broken faces still wear, amidst decay and ruin, the grotesque smile or serene grandeur of their art birth. This cascade and decorations, together with the steps leading to the heights on which they stand, were formerly introduced as "improvements," but are now, perhaps wisely, abandoned to ruin, in which state they certainly have a better effect. We could linger amid these scenes for hours—but there are the kind waving hands of our friends from above. We greet each other kindly, gladness is at the very core of our hearts. Nature has cheered and comforted us; we have come into the clime of birds and bees, and we return with their music in our hearts—return admiring the ferns beautifully luxuriant, and gathering some of them and the red campion, which, spreading everywhere, beautifies the whole extent of the woods.   On our way up the steep which leads back to the castle, we came upon the giant, or " Belted Will," as it is more popularly called, rehearsing as we pass it—

> " When mailed mosstroopers rode the hill,
> When helmed warders paced the keep,
> And bugles blew for Belted Will."

There are many other beauties we have seen and not been able to note at Corby, for our aftenoon was soon gone.   We are, however, bound to pay our tribute of admiration and thanks to the noble owner of all this beauty, whose courtesy and kindness are in fine keeping with this his ancient inheritance.   With the kindly greetings of himself and his, then unbroken, family, we passed by the castle, and, by his own direction, through the gardens, as the nearest way to the station.   We were among the last of our party, and in the dim silence of our own innumerable thoughts, felt devoutly thankful for our afternoon in Corby Walks, and thankful also that this stately home of England, which stands so beautifully on its honoured soil, has for its head a gentleman so truly generous, with an inheritance so largely likely to promote both moral and spiritual refinement.

LINSTOCK, AND LINSTOCK CASTLE.

INSTOCK is a small straggling village, about two miles east of Carlisle, on the north side of the Eden, and closely contiguous to the site of Severus' Wall, one road to it following the direct route of the wall nearly all the way. It has nothing notable about it but its castle; but, leaving Carlisle one beautiful April afternoon, and proceeding thither through Rickerby Holmes, we found a thousand new inspiring charms in the homely irregular beauty of its quiet rural unambitious seclusion, for it really is a very secluded place—no public road, no railway, no noisy works flushing its dreamy nooks with the clash and clatter of earthly care and confusion. The "march of intellect" has certainly left no outward or visible sign of its many-footed train at Linstock, if it has ever been there. It is an old, old place, its cottages and farm-houses following, like antiquated country people, the fashions of very remote and uncouth times, and its gardens and fences generally, too, seem soundly conservative; the pretty simple flowers, which are both eye-salve and heart-salve to meditative loiterers, growing in promiscuous prolixity under a bushy beard-ing of hedge, over which shears surely have never

5

come. Still it has its own wild beauty—a beauty self-assertative and scornful of scorn, the ever-charming green of heartsome nature, which here in common clothing beguiles the varied hour with the common, yet holy joys of morns, and eves, and glowing noons, from which, as from painted pictures, shine all the luminous or shadowy shapes of village life and labour; their noble background the sweeping fields, and fells and river, fringed with all the graceful greenery of a many-aged and many-familied population of trees. There is, in fact, plenty even at Linstock to interest an observing eye and meditative mind for a sunny summer afternoon very often, its castle crowning all its commonplace rusticities with the reverential majesty of memories of princes, and prelates, and noble knights, who once, with all their turbulent tide of attendants, made its quiet corners ring with martial music or loyal cheers. This castle stands at the far end of the village, and is now occupied as a farm-house by Mr. Martindale, who very kindly allowed us to see all, both within and without, that was likely to interest us in it. At present its height is the only thing which makes it observable or conspicuous from the other buildings of the village, as its castellated top has been—very improperly we should say—removed some time since, and replaced by a common tiling, which "improvement," though not ill-suited to its square dimensions, has utterly destroyed any architectural beauty or antique effect it may have had. It is, as we found on coming up to it, beautifully situated for a quiet retreat or secure dwelling, being built on a slight eminence within a very short distance of the Eden, and com-

manding from its strong sides on its third floor very
extensive views of all the country round ; Carlisle and
the Scotland and Newcastle roads lying like an open
map under its ancient brows, and on the south side,
field and fell lie naked and open to it for miles, while
it is so shut in by trees that it is unseen till nearly
reached.   There is also a large stretch of very fertile
country lying all round it, finely fit for raising all sorts
of cereal and vegetable productions for the use of such
a home, and girdling it round at the same time with
leafy lawns, and bowery paths, and pleasant gardens,
where thought of pious or philosophic mood might
pursue its radiant ruminations in supremest peace ;
those "gentle dwellers of the lea," the cowslip, violet,
and primrose, and thousands more of countless forms
and dyes, glowing gladness, pure, bright, and affinitive,
on its mystic visage.

Beyond this quiet, pensive beauty of field and stream,
lying all around it, the castle in itself has little to
boast.   It is a plain, square-built, massive structure of
red sandstone ; a Gothic door or two, and its height
alone, distinguishing its antiquity from the outside.
Inside, the immense thickness of the walls is the most
interesting point.   They are eight or nine feet thick
in many places, a stone staircase having been cut in
the south side, from the second to the third story,
through the breadth of the wall, leaving still a breadth
on both sides equal or more than equal to the thickest
modern walls, a fact pregnant with history—a stony
tome, from which we may gather the perils, and pre-
science, and laborious endeavours of a brave, persistent,
deed-living, deed-loving race, now but too inadequately

represented. The part of the castle now converted into a dairy seems to have undergone the least change. It is entered by one of the above-named Gothic doors, and is on a level with the ground; nevertheless, it seems formerly to have been a cell. It has an arched roof, and at each end there is a long loophole, now glazed, by which, through the thick walls, the shadowy light reaches its interior. There is also, on the right-hand side of the entrance, the form of a door, now built up, which probably in some remote times led to a staircase, or was the opening of a staircase in the wall, by which it communicated with the upper stories. Standing on this floor, reflections of the stormy past come thickly and fast to the mind. Who, in anguish or despair, had trod that narrow space in the older days of the castle? Who, in the mediæval centuries of its existence, had passed and repassed its sombre threshold, waking its weird silence with their piercing prayers or ghostly groans? What fair ladies, and sweet babes, and pleasant homes had been dreamt of at night or thought of by day in that place? What young hearts had wished then that it never were summer, as the golden radiance of June, streaming from afar on the just visible tree-tops, mocked their misery, and brought back blessed but maddening memories?

Whether such sad reflections might not have been true, we will leave our readers to judge from the following facts of the history of this place:—" This castle was the palace of the Bishop of Carlisle till the the 13th January 1229; and about the year 1293, the famous Bishop Hilton is said to have entertained here for a considerable time Johannes Romanus, Archbishop of York, with his train, which amounted to above 300 persons. This prelate was also employed to settle the claims of the pretenders to the Scottish crown, and was present when sentence was given against Robert Bruce, and when John Baliol did homage for the kingdom of Scotland 'to his sovereign lord the King of England.' He was commissioned by the Pope to collect tenths in all the dioceses of Scotland; and in 1302 was Governor of Carlisle Castle, and had charge of all the Scottish hostages and prisoners of note, many of whom, as appears from his papers, *died in durance.* By the orders of Pope Clement V., he, conjointly with the Archbishop of York, in 1305, excommunicated 'by bell, book, and candle,' Robert de Brus, Earl of Carrick, and all his adherents, for the murder of John Comyn in the church of Dumfries. He was present at the Parliament held at Carlisle in 1307, and in the same year was summoned to the coronation of Edward II. He was also in Carlisle in 1314, when that city was blockaded by Edward Bruce. In 1318, Edward II., with the sanction of the Pope, appropriated the church of Horncastle, in Lincolnshire, to the use of Bishop Hilton, as a recompense for his great services, and that he and his successors might have a place of refuge from the Scots. This Bishop was one of the plenipotentiaries in a treaty of peace with Robert de Brus in 1320, but he died in 1324, having held the see thirty-two years."

From this it may be conjectured very fairly that this castle must have been in those past dim times the scene of many stirring events. Bishops were then different in many things from what they are now.

They could don the steel corslet as easily as they could say an *Ave* or a *Paternoster*, and hang or excommunicate, according to the needs of the hour; and this stalwart John Hilton, the owner of Linstock Castle while the fiery Edward I. was at Carlisle, and finished his life and wars on Drumburgh Marsh, a short distance thence, was one of the most martial men of the times. There is little about this castle now to tell of all this; but there must have been other buildings, which were formerly parts of it, right down to the river, for we were told that large stones like old foundations are found by the men employed in weiring the river. There is also a trace of an ancient moat which once ran round its northern side.

We left its peaceful precincts with many thoughts of the far past, its occupants, their lives, their deeds, and how, through the lapsing centuries, all had changed—changed, but still in some palpable manner remaining much the same—the old familiar skies now, as then, shutting down over a beauteous nature—cool breezes, green trees, tender flowers, and the grand gloomy fells. How full of instruction is the past! how full of reverence!—the great need of our times! Well would it be if our masses could better understand these sermons in stones!

Since writing the above we have revisited this " old castle," and find that there are even more points of interest about it than we had at first observed. On the east side more especially there are a great many lights and loopholes now closed up, which formerly did their stint of service to the old place which on that side has not been encumbered with modern additions.

These the curious visitor will note for himself, not forgetting a very aged pear tree on the right of the road he enters by. It is an immense specimen of its kind, seeming a very banyan by the space it covers, and probably in its younger days had the honour of contributing to the general list of good things with which the old bishops so largely supplied their tables. Be this as it may, it is well worth looking at, as it is still healthy and bears, though its huge trunk is all split and torn. It was laden with fruit when we saw it, and a fair haired young urchin, who acted as our guide, all other hands being busy, told us it had produced "a gay few cars full" the year before.

Just Published, price 2s.6d., or with Portrait, 3s.6d.

SONGS AND BALLADS

By JOHN JAMES LONSDALE,

Author of "The Ship Boy's Letter," "Robin's Return," &c.

WITH A BRIEF MEMOIR.

From the *ATHENÆUM, December 21st, 1867.*

Mr. Lonsdale's songs have not only great merit, but they display the very variety of which he himself was sceptical. His first lay, "Minna," might lay claim even to imagination ; nevertheless, for completeness and delicacy of execution, we prefer some of his shorter pieces. Of most of these it may be said that they are the dramatic expressions of emotional ideas. In many cases, however, these songs have the robust interest of story, or that of character and picture. When it is borne in mind that by far the greater portion of these lays were written for music, no small praise must be awarded to the poet, not only for the suitability of his themes to his purpose, but for the picturesqueness and fancy with which he has invested them under difficult conditions.

From the *WESTMINSTER REVIEW, January, 1868.*

Poetry seems now to flourish more in the north than in the south of England. Not long ago we noticed an admirable collection of Cumberland ballads, containing two songs by Miss Blamire, which are amongst the most beautiful and pathetic in our language. We have now a small volume by a Cumberland poet, which may be put on the same shelf with Kirke White. Like Kirke White's, Mr. Lonsdale's life seems to have been marked by pain and disappointment. Like Kirke White too, he died before his powers were full developed. A delicate pathos and a vein of humour characterize his best pieces.

From the *SPECTATOR, January 14th, 1868.*

"The Children's Kingdom" is really touching. The picture of the band of children setting out in the morning bright and happy, lingering in the forest at noon, and creeping to their journey's end at midnight with tearful eyes, has a decided charm.

CARLISLE: GEO. COWARD.

LONDON: ROUTLEDGE AND SONS; AND ALL BOOKSELLERS.

The SONGS and BALLADS of CUMBERLAND,

to which are added Dialect and other Poems; with Biographical Sketches, Notes, and Glossary. Edited by Sidney Gilpin. With Portrait of Miss Blamire. Small Crown 8vo. Price 7s.

One of the most interesting collections of poetry which have been lately published is the "Songs and Ballads of Cumberland." How many people know anything of Miss Blamire? Yet she was the author of that most beautiful and pathetic of ballads beginning, "And ye shall walk in silk attire." Every one will, therefore, thank the editor for the conscientous way in which he has issued her pieces, and given us some account of her life. It was she, too, who wrote that other beautiful ballad, worthy of Lady Anne Lindsay, "What ails this heart o' mine?" which, in our opinion, is poetry full of truth and tenderness. Indeed, we should be disposed to look upon it as a critical touchstone, and to say that those who did not like it could not possibly appreciate true poetry. . . . We can only advise the reader to buy the book, and we feel sure that he, like ourselves, will be thankful to the editor. —*Westminster Review.*

We like the Cumberland Songs a good deal better than the Lancashire ones which we reviewed a fortnight back. There is more go and more variety in them; the hill-air makes them fresher, and we do not wonder that Mr. Gilpin feels—now he has got "tem put in prent"—

Aw England cannot bang them.

We certainly cannot recollect a better collection. . . While the author of "Joe and the Geologist" lives, we shall rest assured that the Cumberland dialect will be well represented in verse as well as prose, though we suppose he cannot love to describe the roaring scenes at weddings and the like that his predecessors witnessed. . . . The dialect is rich in reduplicated words—in good forms—in old English words; and the volume altogether is one that should find a place on the shelf of every reader of poetry and student of manners, customs, and language.— *The Reader.*

The truly Cumbrian minstrel towards the close of the last century seems to have approached the Scotch in his pictures of rural courtship, and to have been still greater in his descriptions of weddings, as of some other festivities of a more peculiar character. He had a healthy and robust standard of feminine beauty, and his most riotous mirth was more athletic and less purely alcoholic than that which flourished in Burns's native soil.—*The Spectator.*

"*Songs and Ballads of Cumberland.*"

These Cumberland lyrics—till now scattered—are on the whole well worth the pains spent on their collection. In some cases, as in those of Relph and Miss Blamire, there is evidence of real genius for the ballad or the eclogue ; and with respect to other writers, if the poetic feeling be less deep, humour and keen observation are displayed in dealing with the people and customs of a district which, in its lingering primitiveness and time-honored traditions, is richer in materials for fancy and character than regions which lie nearer the metropolis.—*The Athenæum.*

It is seldom that a book compiled on the local principle contains so much good matter as this collection of the "Songs and Ballads of Cumberland." In the pathetic vein, Miss Blamire is a host in herself ; and the humorous and "character sketches," as we may call them, by various hands, are more vigorous and picturesque, and less vulgar or coarse, than is at all common in the works of local poets. To some readers the peculiar dialect may be objectionable ; but to any one who can read Burns, it need be no stumbling-block to the enjoyment of the varied contents of this elegant and well-arranged volume. . . The biographical and other notes are carefully and well written, judiciously informative, and not too long.—*Scotsman.*

Cumberland has a goodly store of ballads, the natural off-spring of her hills and lakes, and fells and "forces," a wealth of ballad literature, in fact, whereof the Southron in general knows, we fear, but little. Miss Susanna Blamire is a name of celebrity up North, the poetess of Cumberland ; and Robert Anderson and many others hold almost equal repute there. Mr. Sidney Gilpin, himself owning a name which has belonged to more than one Cumberland celebrity, has collected and edited a volume of the dialect-songs and ballads, and other specimens of the minstrelsy of his county, and offers it to the appreciation of the English public. The "Songs and Ballads of Cumberland" ought to be a welcome volume to all who can relish the home-spun simple language of a genuine muse of the hills. There is much true and tender poetry in the book, and much rough, natural vigour.—*Morning Star.*

Cumberland has found in Mr. Sidney Gilpin an able and zealous champion ; and the present collection of her Songs and Ballads, though not, perhaps, absolutely exhaustive, will decidedly extend her poetic fame, and no doubt surprise many even among the students of this peculiar lore.- *Church and State Review.*

CARLISLE : GEO. COWARD.

LONDON : ROUTLEDGE AND SONS.

MISS BLAMIRE'S SONGS AND POEMS;

together with Songs by her friend MISS GILPIN of Scaleby Castle. With Portrait of Miss Blamire. F. Cap 8vo. Price 2s. 6d.

ROBERT ANDERSON'S CUMBERLAND BALLADS. F. Cap 8vo. Price 2s.

CARLISLE : GEO. COWARD.
LONDON : GEO. ROUTLEDGE AND SONS.

Preparing for Publication,

TALES AND RHYMES IN THE DIALECTS OF CUMBERLAND AND ADJACENT DISTRICTS.

By the Author of "JOE AND THE GEOLOGIST." Small Crown 8vo.

A GLOSSARY OF THE WORDS & PHRASES OF FURNESS, (North Lancashire,) with illustrative quotations, principally from the Old Northern Writers. By J. P. Morris, F.A.S., Cor. Mem. Auth. Soc. of Paris.

JOE & THE GEOLOGIST & "T'REETS ON'T,"

(being a Supplement to "Joe.") Price Twopence.

BOBBY BANKS' BODDERMENT & DIALECT BALLADS. By the Author of "Joe and the Geologist." Price Threepence.

RAYSON'S DIALECT POEMS AND BALLADS.

Complete Edition. F. Cap 8vo. Price 1s.

SIEGE O' BROU'TON. Price 1d.

LEBBY BECK DOBBY. Price 1d.

INVASION O' U'STON. Price 1d.

CARLISLE : GEO. COWARD ; AND ALL BOOKSELLERS
IN CUMBERLAND.

www.ingramcontent.com/pod-product-compliance
Lightning Source LLC
Chambersburg PA
CBHW022143090426
42742CB00010B/1372